THE TRUTH ABOUT MANAGING STUDENT LOAN DEBT

A Real-World Guide to Repayment, Forgiveness, and Freedom

JACQUELINE WILLCOT

Published in the US. ISBN 979-8998888243

Disclaimer:

The information provided in this book is for educational and informational purposes only and does not constitute legal advice. While every effort has been made to ensure accuracy, readers are encouraged to consult with a qualified consumer law attorney or legal professional for advice specific to their individual situation. Laws and regulations may vary by state, and legal guidance should always be sought when dealing with complex credit or debt issues.

Dedication

To Joshua, Lexi, Michael III, and Diamond —

Thank you for being such kind, loving souls. My life is fuller because of each of you. Your laughter warms my heart, your smiles brighten my days, and you are always in my thoughts and prayers. I am incredibly proud of who you are, and all you are becoming.

With all my love,

Mom

Acknowledgments

A Special Note to My Editor

Thank you to my amazing editor, Mary. I'm so grateful for your patience, diligence, and the way you fussed over every little detail to make this book shine. Your sharp eye and steady support made all the difference. You've done an incredible job — thank you so much.

Contents

Introduction

If you're feeling overwhelmed by your student loans, you're not alone. For millions of Americans, student debt isn't just a bill—it's a burden that stretches across years, even decades, impacting credit scores, delaying life milestones, and placing dreams like homeownership, entrepreneurship, or starting a family on hold. The problem isn't just the debt itself. It's the confusion, the silence, the lack of real guidance, and the constantly shifting rules that make it hard to know where to start or what to believe.

But here's the truth: you don't have to wait until the first payment is due to take control. The smartest time to prepare for repayment is before you leave campus. While you're still in school, you can review your loan totals, understand your interest rates, and map out a plan. You can log into StudentAid.gov to see who your servicers are, when your grace period ends, and what repayment options fit your goals. You can contact private lenders directly, start budgeting for life after graduation, and set yourself up with tools that give you confidence instead of panic. Being proactive now can mean the difference between drowning in confusion and stepping into your future with clarity and control.

The Truth About Managing Student Loan Debt is your no-nonsense guide to navigating that journey. It breaks down the differences between federal and private loans, explains how student loans are treated in bankruptcy, and walks you through repayment plans, forgiveness programs, and lesser-known tools that can help you reduce stress, save money, and get your financial footing back.

Whether you are on the verge of graduation, buried in bills, or trying to recover from years of financial setbacks, this book is your guide forward. Inside, you will find the strategies, clarity, and support you need to take control of your debt and reclaim your financial future. You do not need to have all the answers to begin. You just need the truth—honest, empowering, and rooted in the steps that lead to real results.

Please note: This book is for informational purposes only and should not be taken as legal advice. If you're considering bankruptcy or have legal questions about your loans, it's important to speak with a licensed attorney.

Like many people, I had to pay for my college education largely on my own. I received a small amount of grants and scholarships, but it was not nearly enough to cover the full cost of tuition, let alone living expenses. So, I did what millions of others did — borrowed money, hoping it would lead to a better future, and figuring it out as I went, with little guidance on what we were really signing up for.

At one point, I was offered a private consolidation loan with a 2 percent interest rate. That was hard to ignore, especially when my federal loans were sitting at 7.8 percent. The lower rate sounded like the smarter choice. But after doing my research, I realized that converting my federal loans into private debt would mean giving up important protections like income-driven repayment plans, deferment options, and potential loan forgiveness.

I decided not to make the switch. Looking back, it was one of the best financial decisions I ever made. It taught me that student loans are not just about the interest rate. They are about understanding the long-term consequences and knowing what you might lose if you give up federal protections.

This book comes from that experience. I wrote it for people like me — people who borrowed money trying to do the right thing, with little support or clear direction, and who now feel stuck, overwhelmed, or unsure of what to do next. You are not alone in this. There are real options and real answers. And this book is here to help you find both.

ONE

Student Loan Debt

Student loan debt has emerged as one of the most significant consumer debt burdens in the United States, second only to mortgage debt. As of 2024, **approximately 42.7 million Americans carry student loan debt,** accounting for nearly 19 percent of the U.S. adult population aged 18 to 65, or about 1 in every 5 working-age adults. In the United States, some individuals continue to carry their student loan debt well into their later years.

For example, one 91-year-old woman was reported to have more than $300,000 in student loan debt. Whether it is still actively owed or not, the fact that it followed her into her nineties speaks volumes about the long-term weight of these loans.

Estimates place the total outstanding student loan debt at around $1.77 trillion, surpassing the balances held on credit cards (approximately $1.18 trillion) and auto loans (about $1.64 trillion). While mortgage debt remains the largest category of consumer debt in the U.S. at over $12 trillion, student loans are now the second-largest source of household debt. What was once considered a temporary financial tool to open the door to higher education has evolved into a long-term financial obstacle for millions.

The consequences of this rising debt load are profound. Many borrowers find themselves delaying major life milestones, such as buying a home, starting a family, or saving for retirement. For younger borrowers in particular, the weight of student loan payments often competes with basic living expenses, leaving little room for financial growth or security. What was once seen as a smart investment in the future has, for many young adults, turned into a financial burden that delays their ability to build that future.

In the United States, more than 60% of college graduates aged 18 to 23 leave school carrying student loan debt.

TWO

Types of Student Loans

There are two different types of student loans a person can have: **federal loans** and **private loans**. While both are intended to help cover tuition and other educational expenses, federal and private loans differ greatly in structure, regulation, and borrower protections.

Federal student loans are part of a government program administered by the Department of Education under the Federal Direct Loan Program (FDLP). In the past, the federal government also partnered with private lenders through the Federal Family Education Loan Program (FFELP). Although there are minimal differences between the loans issued under each program, no new FFELP loans have originated since 2010. That said, many FFELP loans remain in active repayment or deferment, while all newly issued federal student loans are now made under FDLP.

Both **FDLP** (Federal Direct Loan Program) and **FFELP** (Federal Family Education Loan Program) loans are governed by federal law and come with certain borrower entitlements. These protections are created by Congress and enforced by various offices within the Department of Education to ensure compliance. Key entitlements include:

- **Interest rate caps** to prevent excessive borrowing costs
- **Multiple repayment plan options** tailored to different income levels and financial situations
- **Various deferment options** for qualifying life circumstances such as unemployment, economic hardship, or returning to school

Borrowers facing bankruptcy or financial hardship may also be eligible for additional support through the protections built into these federal loan programs.

Private student loans, on the other hand, operate very differently. Sometimes referred to as alternative loans, they are issued by private sector lenders and are not regulated or administered by the Department of Education. The lender sets the interest rate and repayment terms, which can vary widely from borrower to borrower. While these loans are marketed to help cover educational costs, they are, in effect, unsecured signature loans, and they do not offer the same borrower protections or federal oversight that come with federal student loans. We will explore the key differences between Private versus Federal and important protections associated with federal loans in more detail in the chapters to come.

THREE

Options for Repayment of Federal Loans

If you're having trouble making your student loan payments, one of the best steps you can take is to immediately contact your loan servicer or financing lender to explore options that can help you stay on track. If your debt includes federal student loans, it's often a good idea to start there first. Federal loans typically offer more flexible repayment plans, deferment options, and forgiveness programs as long as the loans **aren't in default**. Knowing your options and acting early can make a big difference in avoiding long-term consequences.

Federal Loan Repayment Options

As long a borrower's loans have not gone into default, the borrower has several repayment options available to them:

- **Standard**
  - Level monthly payments for 10 years (120 months).

Example:

Dee owes $30,000 in federal student loans. Under the Standard Plan, she makes a fixed monthly payment of about $330 for 10 years. After 120 months of consistent payments, her loan is completely paid off. This plan works best for borrowers who can afford higher monthly payments and want to pay their loan off quickly with less interest.

- **Extended**
  - Level monthly payments for up to 25 years (300 months).
  - Available to borrowers with loan balances exceeding $30,000.

Example:

Ashton owes $50,000 in student loans. Because his balance is over $30,000, he qualifies for the Extended Plan. His monthly payments are lowered to around $250 by stretching the repayment over 25 years. While he pays more interest over time, the smaller monthly payments make it more manageable with his current budget.

- **Graduated**
  - Lower monthly payments (as low as interest only) for the first 2-4 years.
  - Payments then increase to cover the loan balance over the remaining term of the loan.

Example:

Addisyn just finished graduate school and started her first job. She owes $40,000 in student loans. She chooses the Graduated Plan, which starts her off with low monthly payments, around

$200 per month, for the first couple of years. As her income increases, so do her payments. By the final years, she'll pay over $500 per month, but the early flexibility helped her stay afloat financially while she builds her career.

- **Income Sensitive**
    - Payment based on a percentage of gross income (4% - 25%).
    - Monthly payment amount must be at least enough to cover the accrued interest for each month.
    - Borrower must apply for this payment plan annually.

Example:

David is a teacher with a starting salary of $38,000. He selects the Income-Sensitive Plan and agrees to pay 10% of his gross monthly income. His monthly student loan payment starts at about $320, just enough to cover the interest. He must reapply each year and submit income documentation to adjust his payments based on his salary changes.

- **Income Based Repayment (IBR)**
    - Borrower must demonstrate financial hardship.
    - Based on a percentage of discretionary income and household size.
    - Repayment can extend up to 25 years.
    - Borrower may be eligible to have loan balances forgiven after 25 years.

Example:

Lovie is a social worker making $35,000 a year and has $60,000 in student loans. She qualifies for **Income-Based Repayment (IBR)**, and her monthly payments are calculated at 10 percent of her discretionary income – the amount of money a person has left to spend or save after paying for essential expenses such as taxes, housing, food, and other necessities; the funds available for non-essential purchases – which works out to be about $150 per month. After 25 years of consistent payments, the remaining balance of her loan may be forgiven.

However, because Lovie works in **public service,** which includes jobs with government agencies, public schools, nonprofit hospitals, and qualifying 501(c)(3) nonprofit organizations, she may qualify for **Public Service Loan Forgiveness (PSLF)**. If she meets all PSLF criteria, including working full-time for a qualifying employer and making 120 monthly payments, her remaining loan balance could be forgiven after just **10 years**.

Student Loan Income-Based Repayment Options

Navigating student loan repayment can be overwhelming, but knowing your options is the first step toward taking control of your debt. This section breaks down the key **Income-Driven Repayment (IDR)** plans to help you choose one that aligns with your financial needs, personal goals, and long-term plans. Whether you're seeking lower monthly payments, more flexibility, or a pathway to loan forgiveness, there's a repayment plan designed to support your journey.

Example:

Dr. Kevin Jones is a pediatrician working at a busy urban hospital. On paper, he's the picture of success: white coat, six-figure salary, and a fulfilling career helping children. But behind the scenes, he's carrying more than just the weight of his patients' needs—he's carrying over $280,000 in student loan debt.

Dr. Jones financed his undergraduate degree, medical school, and living expenses entirely with federal loans. Now, ten years into his practice, the debt hasn't disappeared. In fact, it's barely moved. High interest rates, unexpected medical bills from a family emergency, and the rising cost of living have left him feeling suffocated by a balance that only seems to grow.

Despite his income, the stress is real. He delayed starting a family. He rented longer than he wanted to. He skipped vacations and questioned if he'd ever retire on his own terms.

For years, Kevin felt too overwhelmed—or even embarrassed—to ask for help. But when a close friend shared information about income-driven repayment plans and public service loan forgiveness, he finally took a breath and reached out for guidance.

He learned that by switching his plan and consolidating his loans, he could cut his monthly payment by over $1,000 and stay on track for forgiveness in the future. The emotional relief was immediate.

Although they are currently on a temporary pause as the federal government investigates the legalities of several Income-Driven Repayment (IDR) plans, it is nonetheless important to understand these plans, in hopes that they will be available to help federal student loan borrowers manage their payments again in the future. All three of these plans rely on the borrower's income and family size to determine the amount of their loan repayment. Here's an overview of three key IDR plans:

1. Saving on a Valuable Education (SAVE) Plan

2025 Poverty Guidelines (for all but Alaska and Hawaii)	
Household Size	Poverty Guideline
1	$15,650
2	$21,150
3	$26,650
4	$32,150
5	$37,650
6	$43,150
7	$48,650
8	$54,150

Add $5,500 for each additional family member
(Provided by the Office of the Assistant Secretary
for Planning and Evaluation/https://aspe.hhs.gov)

The SAVE Plan, introduced in 2023, aims to provide more affordable monthly payments and quicker debt relief. Key features include:

- **Payment Calculation:** For undergraduate loans, payments are capped at 5% of discretionary income; for graduate loans, it's 10%. Borrowers with both types have a weighted average between 5% and 10%.

- **Discretionary Income Definition:** Income above 225% of the federal poverty guideline is considered discretionary, allowing more borrowers to qualify for $0 monthly payments.

- **Interest Accrual:** Unpaid interest is not added to the loan balance, so the loan balance doesn't continue to grow while the borrower is paying on it.

- **Forgiveness:** Borrowers with original principal balances of $12,000 or less may receive forgiveness after 10 years of payments. Borrowers with larger balances may achieve forgiveness after 20 or 25 years, depending on the loan type.

Example:

Taylor is a teacher earning $42,000 a year and has $11,000 in federal undergraduate student loans. Under the SAVE Plan, her payment is calculated at 5 percent of her discretionary income, or about $90 per month. Because her original loan was under $12,000, she may qualify for full forgiveness after just 10 years of consistent payments and she won't have to worry about her balance growing due to unpaid interest.

2. Pay As You Earn (PAYE) Plan

The PAYE Plan – Pay As You Earn – is designed for borrowers who are experiencing partial financial hardships. Key aspects of the PAYE Plan include:

- **Payment Calculation:** Monthly payments are 10% of discretionary income, but never more than the 10-year Standard Repayment Plan amount.

- **Eligibility:** The PAYE Plan is available to borrowers who took out their first federal student loan after October 1, 2007, and received a disbursement of a Direct Loan on or after October 1, 2011. Additionally, the borrower must demonstrate a partial financial hardship to qualify for this plan, which means that the monthly amount they would be required to pay under the Standard 10-year repayment plan is higher than what they would pay under the PAYE Plan, based on their income and family size.

- **Forgiveness:** Any remaining loan balance is forgiven after 20 years of qualifying payments.

Example:

Travis graduated in 2012 with $45,000 in student loans and earns $38,000 a year. Because he meets the date and income eligibility rules, he qualifies for PAYE. His monthly payment is about $120, based on 10 percent of his discretionary income. After 20 years of consistent payments, any remaining balance may be forgiven.

3. Income-Contingent Repayment (ICR) Plan

Unlike the SAVE and PAYE plans, the ICR Plan is the only IDR option available to Parent PLUS Loan borrowers (after consolidation). In general, this plan is not as beneficial as the SAVE and PAYE plans because it has a higher payment cap and longer repayment period. Its features include:

- **Payment Calculation:** Monthly payments are the lesser of 20% of discretionary income or what you would pay on a fixed 12-year repayment plan, adjusted for income.

- **Discretionary Income Definition:** Income above 100% of the federal poverty guideline is considered discretionary.

- **Forgiveness:** Loan forgiveness is granted after 25 years of qualifying payments.

Example:

Kameron took out Parent PLUS Loans to help her child through college. After consolidating the loans into a Direct Consolidation Loan, she enrolls in the ICR Plan. Her payments are based on 20 percent of her discretionary income, which comes to around $280 per month. She can qualify for forgiveness after 25 years of payments. If Kameron had chosen to repay her original Parent PLUS Loan under the Standard 10-Year Repayment Plan without consolidating, her monthly payment would have been approximately $596, and she would have paid off the loan in full after 10 years, with a total repayment of around $71,520—but without any forgiveness.

Public Service Loan Forgiveness

PSLF (Public Service Loan Forgiveness) is a federal program that forgives the remaining balance on Direct federal student loans after a qualifying borrower has:

- Made 120 qualifying monthly payments;

- While working full-time;

- For a qualifying public service employer.

Who Is Eligible for PSLF?

To qualify for PSLF, a borrower must have direct loans (Subsidized, Unsubsidized, Grad PLUS, Consolidation Loans). If the borrower has a **Federal Family Education Loan (FFEL)** or Perkins loans, those must be first consolidated into a Direct Consolidation Loan. Additionally, the borrower must be an employee of:

- **Government organizations** (federal, state, local, or tribal)

- **501(c)(3) nonprofit organizations**

- Certain **nonprofit organizations** that qualifying public services (like public health, education, or law enforcement)

Employment Requirements:

The borrower must also meet basic employment requirements, including:

- Work full-time (at least 30 hours/week or meet your employer's full-time definition, whichever is greater)

- Can work for multiple qualifying employers simultaneously to meet full-time status

Payment Requirements:

The borrower must make 120 monthly payments (do not have to be consecutive), under the PSLF. Those payments must be:

- On time;

- Made under a qualifying repayment plan (like Income-Driven Repayment—SAVE, PAYE, REPAYE, or IBR;

- For Direct Loans only (FFEL and Perkins loans must be consolidated first.)

Forgiveness Terms:

- After 120 qualifying payments, the remaining loan balance is completely forgiven

- Forgiveness is not taxable under current IRS rules

Example:

Davita is a nurse working full-time at a nonprofit hospital. She has $70,000 in Direct Loans and makes consistent payments under the SAVE Plan. After working in public service for 10 years and making 120 qualifying payments, the rest of her loan balance is forgiven tax-free under PSLF.

The Income Driven Repayment (IDR) Account Adjustment is a one-time initiative introduced by the U.S. Department of Education in 2022 to correct long standing errors in how federal student loan repayment histories have been tracked. This effort is part of a broader campaign to ensure borrowers receive appropriate credit toward loan forgiveness under both IDR plans and the Public Service Loan Forgiveness (PSLF) program.

Over the years, poor servicing practices led to many borrowers being misinformed, steered into forbearance, or placed into deferment instead of income-driven repayment plans. These missteps delayed forgiveness for millions, even among those who consistently tried to stay in good standing.

The IDR adjustment seeks to correct those missteps by retrospectively applying qualifying credit for time that was previously not counted. These corrections are being automatically applied to eligible federal loans, helping many borrowers move significantly closer to full loan forgiveness.

New Qualifying Periods Toward Forgiveness

Traditionally, only active repayment under an income driven repayment plan—or payments made while working for a qualifying employer under PSLF—would count toward loan forgiveness. However, the IDR Account Adjustment expands what qualifies, acknowledging that many borrowers were unfairly excluded due to system errors or poor guidance.

Borrowers will now receive credit for:

- Any months in repayment, regardless of the repayment plan or whether payments were made in full or on time

- Forbearance periods of 12 or more consecutive months, or 36 or more months total

- Economic hardship deferment after 2013

- Military service deferment

- Months in qualifying deferment or forbearance prior to consolidation

- COVID 19 emergency forbearance

Note: While many deferments now count, in-school deferments and grace periods are excluded from forgiveness credit under this adjustment.

These expanded rules provide long overdue relief to borrowers who may have otherwise spent decades repaying loans without ever seeing meaningful progress toward cancellation.

What Borrowers Need to Do

Borrowers with Direct Loans will automatically receive these adjustments. Those with FFEL, Perkins, or other non-Direct federal loans must consolidate into a Direct Loan to become eligible. Deadlines for consolidation may apply, so timely action is critical.

For many long-term borrowers, especially those in public service or those who entered repayment 20 or more years ago, this adjustment may result in immediate or near-term loan forgiveness.

The heavy weight that many students carry long after graduation, the burden of debt can become too much for young adults struggling to become financially independent or older adults who have experienced a financial setback from an unexpected life event or tragedy. Seeking help navigating the maze of student loans repayment options can feel intimidating or even shameful. When life becomes challenging, it can be tempting to push student loan payments to the back burner and forget about them. We get it. You're not alone. Let's walk through the terms, consequences, programs, and legalities together to give you the knowledge to make informed decisions.

I've been paying on my student loans for years. Like so many others, there were times when I was able to stay on track, and other times when life got in the way. I had to rely on deferments and forbearances just to make it through certain seasons. That pushed my repayment out much longer than I ever expected.

By the time I really started looking into my options, I had already been out of school for 18 years. During that time, the interest had continued to build — and my loan balance had nearly tripled from the original amount I borrowed.

I spent seven of those years working for a nonprofit. I loved the work and the opportunity to serve others. So when I found out I was just three years short of qualifying for Public Service Loan Forgiveness, I was disappointed — and honestly, somewhat lost and confused about what to do next.

When the IDR account adjustment was introduced, I realized there might still be a path forward. Some of my older payments and even time in deferment could now count toward forgiveness. But it wasn't automatic. I had to consolidate my loans, apply for the adjustment, and make sure every step was completed correctly.

Eventually, I received forgiveness.

It took persistence, patience, and a willingness to advocate for myself. But it happened. And that kind of relief is real — and every borrower should have the chance to take back control, reclaim their peace, and move forward without shame or confusion.

Delinquency vs. Default: Understanding the Difference

When it comes to student loans, it's important to understand the difference between delinquency and default—especially since these terms are often used interchangeably in other types of lending.

In many lending sectors, being behind on payments may automatically be considered a default. In other words, if you miss payments, the lender may assume you do not intend to repay the debt.

However, federal student loans have a more specific and structured process. If you miss a payment, your loan is first considered delinquent. This status begins the first day after a missed payment and continues until the payment is made or alternative arrangements are established.

If the loan remains unpaid for 270 days (about nine months), it is then classified as in default.

This distinction matters. As long as your federal loan is in delinquency—not yet in default—you may still have access to valuable options, including:

- Repayment plan adjustments
- Deferment or forbearance
- Loan rehabilitation or consolidation

Taking action during the delinquency phase can help you avoid the serious consequences of default, such as damage to your credit, wage garnishment, or legal collection efforts.

Forbearance & Deferment

Deferment allows you to legally postpone your loan payments for a specific period without penalty. In many cases, no interest will accrue during this time if you have subsidized federal loans.

Subsidized loans are a type of federal student loan in which the government pays the interest on your behalf while you are:

- Enrolled in school at least half-time

- In your six-month grace period after leaving school

- Approved for a qualified deferment period

This makes subsidized loans more affordable than unsubsidized loans, which begin accruing interest immediately after they are disbursed. Even if you're in school or deferment, the interest on unsubsidized loans continues to grow and is typically added to your loan balance if not paid, causing your debt to increase over time.

You may qualify for deferment based on specific situations, such as:

- Being enrolled in school at least half-time
- Active military duty
- Experiencing unemployment or economic hardship

If you meet the eligibility criteria, you are entitled to deferment, and your loan servicer must approve it.

Forbearance also allows you to pause or reduce your loan payments for a temporary period, but it works differently from the deferment. **During forbearance, interest continues to accrue on all types of loans, including subsidized ones.** This means your loan balance will grow unless you pay the interest as it accrues.

Forbearance is generally granted at the discretion of your loan servicer, and is designed for short-term financial struggles, such as:

- Temporary financial hardship
- Medical emergencies
- Natural disasters
- Other unexpected life events

Forbearance can be a helpful short-term tool, but it should be used with caution. **Because interest continues to add up, extended use of forbearance can significantly increase your total repayment amount.**

Bottom Line

Both deferment and forbearance can help you avoid delinquency or default during challenging times, but they are not long-term solutions. Deferment is typically the better option if you qualify, especially if you have subsidized loans, because it can save you money on interest.

If you're unsure which option is right for you, speak with your loan servicer. Taking a proactive approach to managing your student loans, even during hard times, can keep you in the best position to regain control and move forward.

Types of Federal Student Loan Deferment

Federal student loan deferment allows qualified borrowers to temporarily pause payments without going into default. Here are some of the most common types of deferment, along with eligibility guidelines and important considerations:

In-School Deferment

You may qualify for an in-school deferment if you are enrolled at least half-time in a college, university, or eligible trade school. Each institution defines "half-time" differently, but it typically means taking at least six credit hours per semester at the under-graduate level.

- No time limit applies as long as you remain enrolled at least half-time.
- Interest does not accrue on subsidized loans during this deferment.
- Interest does accrue on unsubsidized loans unless you choose to pay it.

Example:

Dennis is working toward his associate degree and takes two night classes each semester while working full-time. Because he is enrolled in six credit hours per term, he qualifies for an in-school deferment and is not required to make payments on his subsidized federal loans while in school.

Unemployment Deferment

If you are unemployed and actively seeking work, you may be eligible for an unemployment deferment.

- Eligibility lasts for up to 36 months.
- You must reapply regularly and provide documentation showing your job search efforts or unemployment status.
- Subsidized loans do not accrue interest during this time; unsubsidized loans do.

Economic Hardship Deferment

Borrowers experiencing significant financial difficulty, including those filing for bankruptcy or receiving public assistance, may qualify for this deferment.

- Available for up to 36 months total.
- Requires documentation of income and expenses or proof of public assistance.
- Interest rules follow the same pattern: subsidized loans are interest-free; unsubsidized loans continue to accrue interest.

Military Service Deferment

If you are serving in the U.S. Armed Forces during a war, military operation, or national emergency, you may qualify for a military service deferment on your federal student loans. This benefit helps relieve the financial pressure of loan payments during your service.

This deferment can also apply to certain National Guard members and to borrowers returning from active duty.

Who Qualifies

You may be eligible for military deferment if you meet any of the following:

- You are on active duty during a war, national emergency, or military operation.
- You are performing qualifying National Guard duty during the same conditions.
- After returning from active duty, you may receive up to 13 additional months of deferment, or until you re-enroll at least half-time in an eligible school, whichever comes first.

How Interest Works During Military Deferment

- **Subsidized Loans**: No interest accrues during the deferment period.
- **Unsubsidized Loans**: Interest does accrue, unless you qualify for additional military interest waivers through programs like the Servicemembers Civil Relief Act (SCRA).

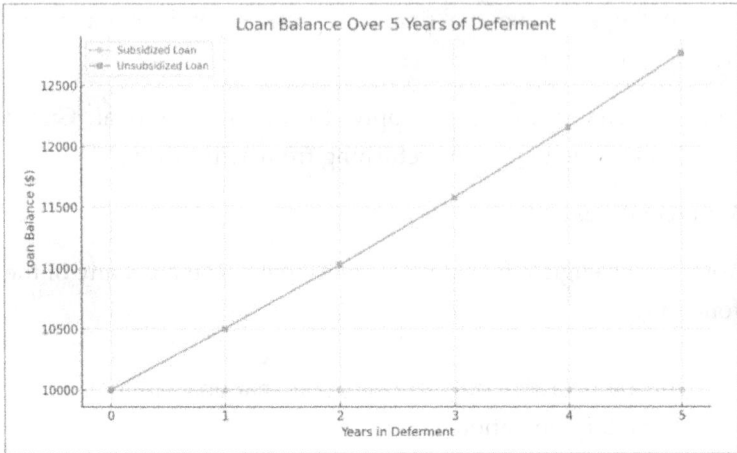

Loan Balance Over 5 Years of Deferment

When the Deferment Starts and Ends

- The deferment starts on the first day of your qualifying service.
- It ends 180 days after your active-duty service is completed, unless you resume school or qualify for post-active-duty deferment.

Documentation You'll Need

To apply for a military deferment, you must submit one of the following to your loan servicer:

- A copy of your military orders
- A written statement from your commanding or personnel officer
- A completed Military Service and Post-Active-Duty Student Deferment Request form signed by an authorized official

Total and Permanent Disability (TPD) Discharge Program

Veterans with a 100% service-connected disability, or those rated totally disabled due to unemployability, may qualify to have their federal student loans, including Parent PLUS, forgiven through the Total and Permanent Disability (TPD) Discharge program. You can apply directly via the TPD portal at StudentAid.gov using VA disability documentation. If approved, your remaining loan balance is canceled, and payments made after your disability date may be refunded. Visit StudentAid.gov for more information.

Important Note

Federal guidelines clearly define eligibility, but loan servicers may apply the rules differently. Some may automatically approve deferment for all active-duty members, while others may only apply it to those who are deployed or in combat zones.

Always check directly with your servicer to confirm their interpretation and make sure you provide all required documentation.

Example:

Sergeant Michael Vent was deployed overseas as part of a military operation. While on active duty, he applied for a military deferment by submitting his deployment orders. His loan servicer approved the deferment, and no payments were required during his service. Since he had subsidized federal loans, no interest accrued during this period.

After returning home, Michael received an additional 13-month deferment to adjust to civilian life and explore educational opportunities. This gave him time to re-enroll in school without falling behind on his loans.

Understanding Forbearance

Forbearance refers to the temporary suspension or reduction of student loan payments, typically due to financial hardship. In the context of student loans, it means the lender or servicer agrees to temporarily pause collection efforts on a debt that is still legally owed.

Definitions

Forbearance: The act of refraining from a legal right.

For federal student loans, forbearance may be granted when a borrower does not meet the eligibility requirements for a deferment. For example, a borrower who is going through bankruptcy may not be enrolled in school, serving in the military, or unemployed—all of which are typical qualifications for deferment. Even though bankruptcy suggests financial distress, having a steady income could disqualify the borrower from receiving a deferment.

In such cases, forbearance may be offered at the discretion of the loan servicer. This allows the borrower to suspend or reduce payments for a limited time, typically in three-month increments. Most federal loan servicers impose a lifetime maximum of 36 months of forbearance per loan, though terms may vary.

Forbearance - Private Student Loans:

While **private lenders** may use the term "deferment" in their documentation, what they offer is usually a form of forbearance, not a true deferment as defined by federal standards. This distinction matters.

Unlike federal deferments, private loan forbearance is not guaranteed. It is entirely at the discretion of the lender, meaning the borrower has no legal right or entitlement to receive it.

Availability, terms, and interest accrual policies vary significantly by lender. Some private lenders may offer temporary payment relief during in-school periods, unemployment, or financial hardship, but these policies are not standardized and often come with strict conditions.

Borrowers with private loans should carefully review their promissory note or contact their lender directly to understand whether any hardship options exist and what the consequences of using them might be—especially since interest almost always continues to accrue during private loan forbearance periods.

Interest Rates During Deferment and Forbearance on Private Loans

Private student loan interest accrual does not follow the same rules as federal loans. They often carry higher, variable interest rates and lack borrower protections like subsidized interest during deferment. Many private lenders use the term "deferment," but what they offer is usually a form of discretionary forbearance, where interest always accrues and the borrower is responsible for paying it.

Because private lenders are not required to offer standardized relief options, interest can accumulate rapidly—especially if a borrower is facing bankruptcy, illness, or other financial hardships. This makes private loan balances harder to manage without a structured repayment plan.

As of recent data:

- **Private student loan interest rates typically range from 4 to 16 percent**, depending on the borrower's credit and lender terms.
- **Federal student loan interest rates are fixed and lower** —around 5.5 percent for undergraduate loans and up to

8.05 percent for PLUS loans in the 2024–2025 academic year.

Key facts about private student loans:

- Interest accrues during all payment pauses, regardless of the reason
- Most private loans offer no income-driven repayment or forgiveness programs
- Unpaid interest is usually capitalized, increasing the total balance owed
- Loan terms and relief options vary widely by lender
- Paying at least the monthly interest during deferment or forbearance can help prevent runaway debt growth

Understanding how interest works on private loans is critical. Without the protections available to federal borrowers, staying proactive is the best way to minimize long-term costs.

Example:

Darra was granted a temporary forbearance from her private lender. Rather than ignore the loan during that time, she made small monthly payments to cover the interest—around $40 each month. Because she stayed on top of the accruing interest, her loan balance did not grow out of control. When regular payments resumed, her balance was nearly the same as when she paused, helping her stay on track and avoid long-term financial strain.

Tip

If your loan is in deferment or forbearance, paying just the monthly interest, even a small amount, can make a big difference in preventing runaway debt.

Interest Rates During Deferment and Forbearance on Federal Student Loans

Understanding how interest accrues during periods of deferment or forbearance is essential to managing the long-term cost of your federal student loans. These pauses in repayment can provide short-term relief during times of hardship, but they affect each loan type differently—and may lead to higher balances if not managed carefully.

Federal Student Loans fall into two main categories when it comes to interest treatment: subsidized and unsubsidized.

Subsidized Stafford Loans and Federal Perkins Loans:

If you qualify for a deferment, the federal government will pay the interest on these loans during the deferment period. This means your loan balance remains unchanged while your payments are paused. However, this protection does not apply during forbearance. If you enter forbearance, interest begins to accrue immediately, and you are responsible for paying it. If left unpaid, this interest can be capitalized—added to the loan balance—once repayment resumes.

Unsubsidized Stafford Loans, Direct Consolidation Loans, Grad PLUS Loans, and Parent PLUS Loans:

These loans accrue interest during both deferment and forbearance. The government does not cover interest for these loans under any payment pause, and borrowers are fully responsible for all accrued interest. If you do not pay this interest while your loan is paused, it will also be capitalized at the end of the deferment or forbearance period, increasing your principal balance and the total amount of interest you'll pay in the future.

Key points to remember:

- Only subsidized loans are eligible for interest relief during deferment
- Forbearance never includes interest subsidies—interest accrues on all loan types
- Unpaid interest may be capitalized, increasing your total loan balance
- Paying interest as it accrues can prevent your debt from growing unnecessarily
- Refinancing a private loan with another private lender may result in a lower interest rate.

Being informed about how deferment and forbearance affect interest accumulation helps you make smarter decisions, especially when weighing short-term relief against long-term cost. Where possible, consider paying the interest during these periods to avoid unnecessary debt growth.

Paying Interest as It Accrues

In both deferment and forbearance, borrowers have the option to pay the interest monthly while their payments are paused. Doing so prevents *capitalization*, which occurs when unpaid interest is added to the principal loan balance at the end of the deferment or forbearance period. Moreover, capitalization increases the total amount you owe and causes interest to be charged on a higher balance moving forward.

Example:

Diamond worked in her chosen field for five years after graduation. When her husband received a job promotion that required relocating, the family moved to another state. Shortly after the move, Diamond gave birth to their second child. With a newborn at home and limited childcare options, it took nearly a year for her to reenter the workforce.

During that time, her student loan payments became difficult to manage on a single income. Feeling the financial pressure, Diamond contacted her student loan servicer and was granted a temporary forbearance.

The pause in payments gave her space to focus on her family and adjust to the new circumstances. Determined not to let her loan balance spiral, she chose to pay the monthly interest—around $45—while her regular payments were on hold. By doing so, she prevented the unpaid interest from being added to her principal balance through capitalization.

Although the forbearance was not ideal, it gave Diamond time to regain stability without letting her debt grow out of control. When she returned to work, her loan balance was nearly unchanged, and she was able to shift into a more manageable repayment plan that fit her new lifestyle

FOUR

Defaulted Loans

A default occurs when it is determined that the borrower has failed to repay their student loan and attempts to collect the debt have not been successful. With federal student loans, the conditions for default are clearly defined. For private student loans, the conditions are set by the individual lender as outlined in the promissory note.

Federal Loan Defaults

A federal student loan is considered in default when a borrower goes 270 days without making a scheduled payment. At that point, the loan status changes from **delinquent** to **defaulted**. For the loan holder, this change allows them to pursue reimbursement from the federal government under the terms of the loan guarantee. Depending on when the loan was disbursed, the lender — typically a bank or private financial institution in older federally backed loans — may be reimbursed for 97 percent to 100 percent of the outstanding principal and interest.

For the borrower, the consequences are more severe. They will lose all entitlements related to repayment programs, deferments, and future federal student aid eligibility. The loan is typically transferred to a guaranty agency and often outsourced to a private collection agency.

The collection agency has the legal authority to:

- Demand full repayment of the loan
- Initiate income tax refund offsets through the federal government
- Garnish wages at a rate of up to 15 percent of gross income
- Garnish Social Security Disability and retirement income

> **Definitions**
>
> **Guaranty Agency: is a state agency, private nonprofit organization, or private sector company authorized to guarantee student loans under the Higher Education Act.**

Importantly, there is no statute of limitations on federal student loan collections, meaning the debt can be pursued indefinitely.

While default can worsen an already difficult financial situation, especially for someone going through bankruptcy, there are still potential options for relief. Bankruptcy filers with defaulted federal loans may be able to explore certain recovery or resolution paths, which will be discussed in the following section.

Rehabilitation of a Defaulted Loan: What It Really Means

Rehabilitating a student loan isn't just about making payments— it's about reclaiming your financial footing and restoring access to federal benefits lost during default. When a federal student loan goes into default, the entire balance becomes due immediately. Borrowers lose eligibility for deferment, income-driven repayment plans, loan forgiveness programs, and federal financial aid. In addition, the default is reported to national credit bureaus, which can severely damage your credit and lead to wage garnishment, tax refund offsets, and persistent collection activity.

Loan rehabilitation provides a one-time opportunity for federal student loan borrowers to restore their loans to good standing. By successfully completing a structured repayment plan, typically nine on time monthly payments based on income, the default status is removed from their credit report. While previous delinquencies may still appear, removing the default can significantly improve credit standing and restore eligibility for federal loan benefits.

How Federal Student Loan Rehabilitation Works

Although collection agencies have the right to demand full repayment, they usually understand that most borrowers cannot pay the full amount at once. Instead, they may offer rehabilitation as a solution.

Here's how it works:

- The borrower contacts the collection agency and requests to rehabilitate the defaulted loan.
- The agency gathers information about the borrower's income, living expenses, and financial obligations to calculate an affordable monthly payment.
- If the borrower feels the proposed amount is unaffordable, they may submit documentation to request a lower payment.

- Once the plan is agreed upon, the borrower must make nine on-time monthly payments within ten months.

After successfully completing the rehabilitation:

- The loan is removed from default and transferred to a new loan servicer.
- The borrower regains access to federal benefits, including deferment, forbearance, income-driven repayment plans, and eligibility for federal student aid.
- Most importantly, the default status is removed from the borrower's credit report

How "Default" Appears on Your Credit Report

Before rehabilitation—defaulted federal student loans are typically reported to the credit bureaus as:

- **In collections** or **in default**, signaling serious delinquency
- **Delinquent**, with missed payments reported for several months leading up to the default
- **Damaging to credit scores**, often resulting in a significant drop depending on the borrower's overall credit history

After successful rehabilitation:

- The **default status is removed** from your credit report, which can help improve your overall credit standing
- However, **late payments and delinquencies that occurred before the default** will **remain on your credit report** for up to **seven years** from the date of the first missed payment

This distinction is important. While rehabilitation erases the label of default, it does **not wipe the full history of late payments** leading up to it. Still, removing the default can make a meaningful difference when applying for **new credit, renting housing, or passing employment-related credit checks**. It also restores eligibility for federal benefits such as income-driven repayment plans, deferment, and loan forgiveness programs.

Example:

Tiffany's student loan went into collections. The collection agency was aggressively contacting him to pay the full amount. At first, she ignored the calls, but eventually, she answered and expressed a desire to fix the situation. The agent explained the rehabilitation process and helped Tiffany agree to a monthly payment that fit her budget.

Tiffany completed the nine required on-time payments. As a result:

- Her loan was removed from default
- She was transferred to a new loan servicer
- She became eligible for income-driven repayment plans and deferments
- The default mark was removed from his credit report, though the prior late payments remained

Thanks to rehabilitation, Tiffany not only regained control over her student debt but also improved her financial standing and credit outlook.

Important Considerations

- Rehabilitation is a one-time opportunity. Once used, you cannot rehabilitate the same loan again if it goes back into default.

- The default status is removed from your credit report, but the late payments that led to default may remain for up to seven years.
- After rehabilitation, you are free to explore long-term repayment solutions such as income-driven plans to prevent future default.

Private Student Loans

Private student loans, typically used to fill funding gaps when federal aid isn't enough, must comply with general consumer protection and banking laws, but do not follow federal student loan rules. Private lending institutions – banks, credit unions, or online financial companies – sets their own rules based on the borrower's credit profile. This leads to a wide variety of loan conditions and non-standardized terms.

For example:

- Interest rates may be **fixed** or **variable**
- Borrowing limits and repayment terms differ by lender
- Fees, penalties, and relief options vary widely

One important similarity to federal loans is that most private student loans cannot be discharged in bankruptcy. This legal protection benefits lenders and reflects the assumption that student borrowers may not have steady income immediately after school. However, there is growing interest in reforming bankruptcy laws to allow private student loan discharge in extreme financial hardship—this topic is explored later in the book.

Repayment Challenges and Default Options for Private Loans

Private loans usually carry higher interest rates than federal loans, which means they can grow quickly, especially if a borrower delays payments or enters hardship.

Unlike federal loan servicers, private lenders are not required to offer flexible repayment plans. This can make it difficult for struggling borrowers to stay current. When a private loan goes into default, the borrower typically has two limited options:

1. Negotiate a lump-sum settlement
2. Request a modified repayment plan

Settlement

If you're in default and can offer a lump sum, many lenders will negotiate a reduced payoff amount. This can help close the debt quickly—but it requires access to cash that most struggling borrowers don't have. In some cases, lenders may also accept short-term repayment plans as part of a settlement.

Modified Payment Plan

Some private lenders may agree to a lower monthly payment if you can show proof of financial hardship. However, these agreements are not guaranteed, and even the reduced payment may still be unaffordable depending on the size of your loan.

In desperation, some borrowers send small payments—just to avoid collection calls or letters. While this may slow down aggressive communication, it often leads to negative amortization, where payments don't even cover the interest, and the loan balance keeps growing.

Why Private Loan Collections Are Tougher

Private lenders tend to be more aggressive than federal servicers when collecting on defaulted loans. This is because private loans are not federally insured—so if the borrower defaults, the lender absorbs the loss. In contrast, federal lenders can often recover funds from the government.

Because of this, private lenders may pursue borrowers more forcefully, using:

- Frequent phone calls
- Letters and emails
- Intense pressure to settle

They can also file a lawsuit to collect the debt. But unlike federal lenders, they must first sue the borrower in court and win a judgment before they can garnish wages or seize funds. This legal process is time-consuming and costly, so lenders often attempt aggressive collection tactics before taking legal action.

Even though private lenders may be more aggressive, they are still bound by the Fair Debt Collection Practices Act (FDCPA) if they use a third-party collection agency. This law protects you from harassment, threats, or deceptive practices. If a collector crosses the line—calling excessively, using abusive language, or misrepresenting the debt—you have the right to report them. You can file a complaint with the Consumer Financial Protection Bureau (CFPB) or your state attorney general's office. You may also choose to hire a consumer protection attorney who specializes in debt collection violations. If your rights have been violated, you could be entitled to recover up to $1,000 in statutory damages, plus the attorney's fees and court costs. You don't have to tolerate mistreatment, even if you owe the debt.

Key Takeaway

Private student loans are often less forgiving and more expensive than federal loans—especially once they go into default. If you are struggling with private loan debt, your options are limited, but not impossible. Communication, documentation, and negotiation are essential tools when dealing with private lenders. In some cases, seeking legal or credit counseling support may be necessary.

Getting Out of Default: Federal Student Loans

If you've defaulted on a federal student loan, you have **two main options** to get back in good standing: **loan consolidation** and **loan rehabilitation**. Each offers different benefits and outcomes depending on your goals.

Option 1: Loan Consolidation

You can consolidate a defaulted federal loan into a new **Direct Consolidation Loan**, which pays off your old loan and creates a new one. This option can restore eligibility for federal benefits quickly.

To qualify, you must either:

- Make **three** on-time, voluntary monthly payments to the collection agency handling your loan, then apply for consolidation,

OR

- Agree to repay the new loan under an **income-driven repayment (IDR) plan** such as:
  - Income-Based Repayment (IBR)
  - Pay As You Earn (PAYE)
  - Saving on a Valuable Education (SAVE)

Choosing an IDR plan often allows you to bypass the three-payment requirement and consolidate right away.

What Consolidation Does:

- Brings your loan current
- Stops wage garnishment and other collection efforts
- Restores eligibility for:
    - Federal student aid
    - Deferment and forbearance
    - IDR plans and forgiveness programs

What It Doesn't Do:

- Does not remove the default status from your credit report
- The record of default may remain for up to seven years from the original delinquency date

Option 2: Loan Rehabilitation

If your goal is to improve your credit, loan rehabilitation is the better choice. It requires you to make **nine on-time monthly payments** (within ten months) based on your income and expenses.

Benefits of Rehabilitation:

- **Removes the default notation** from your credit report
- Restores access to all federal benefits
- Allows for future consolidation if desired

Example:

Tyra defaulted on her student loans after a job loss. When she found new employment, she wanted to return to school and qualify for financial aid. She chose **rehabilitation**, made nine affordable payments, and had the default removed from her credit report. Later, she consolidated her loan to simplify repayment going forward.

Getting Out of Default: Private Student Loans

Unlike federal loans, **private student loans** do not offer standardized programs like consolidation or rehabilitation through the Department of Education. Instead, your options depend on the **policies of your specific lender.**

1. Settlement or Negotiated Repayment
   - Many private lenders are willing to negotiate a lump-sum payoff for less than the full amount owed, especially if the account has been in default for a long time. Settling the debt can help you avoid litigation and stop collection activity, but it may still impact your credit report. Additionally, if a portion of the loan is forgiven or canceled through settlement, the amount forgiven may be considered taxable income by the IRS. This means you could receive a 1099-C form and owe taxes on the forgiven balance, even though you didn't actually receive that money in cash. It's important to speak with a tax professional before finalizing any settlement agreement.
2. Refinancing
   - If your credit has improved or you have a co-signer, you may qualify to **refinance** your private loans with a new lender. Refinancing a defaulted loan is rare, but possible with some online or credit union lenders.
3. Lawsuits and Judgments
   - Private lenders must sue and win a court judgment before garnishing your wages or seizing assets. However, once they obtain a judgment, they can pursue more aggressive collection methods. *Each state has its own statute of limitations that limits how long a*

creditor has to file a lawsuit for unpaid debt. If the deadline passes, they may still try to collect, but they can no longer take legal action.

Important Note on Collections

Private loan servicers are not subject to the same rules as federal servicers. However, if the loan is sent to a third-party collector, **you are protected under the Fair Debt Collection Practices Act (FDCPA).**

FDCPA Protections Include:

- No harassment, threats, or false claims
- Right to request debt validation
- Ability to limit or stop collector contact in writing

FIVE

Settlement of Federal Student Loans

While it's extremely rare, it is possible to settle a federal student loan for less than the full amount owed. The U.S. Department of Education and its loan servicers generally do not accept settlement offers unless the loan has been in default for a long time, and all other collection efforts have failed.

Settlements are typically considered only in extreme financial hardship cases or when the debt is deemed legally uncollectible, such as when the borrower is seriously ill, has no income, or is permanently disabled.

Types of Federal Loan Settlements

When federal loan settlements are approved, they usually fall into one of these three categories:

1. **Waiving collection costs only**
   - You still pay the full principal and interest but avoid additional fees.

2. **Paying the principal plus part of the interest**
   ○ You may receive a partial interest reduction but are still responsible for the original loan amount.
3. **Paying less than the total balance**
   ○ This is extremely rare and usually reserved for cases where the borrower is judgment-proof (unable to pay anything due to long-term hardship).

What a Settlement Means for Your Credit

Even if you settle, the missed payments and default status will remain on your credit report for up to seven years. The loan will also be marked as "settled" rather than "paid in full," which may negatively affect your credit score.

However, for some borrowers, the relief of resolving a long-standing debt outweighs the credit consequences, especially if the debt has already damaged their credit for years.

Example:

Alexis defaulted on her federal student loans over a decade ago. She had been out of work for years due to chronic illness and had no assets or income. Collection agencies had repeatedly contacted her, but she simply couldn't afford any form of payment.

Eventually, the loan servicer offered her a settlement of 85% of the principal balance—waiving collection fees and some interest. Alexis was able to borrow the lump sum from a family member and accepted the offer. While the default remained on her credit report, she was no longer receiving collection calls, and her overall debt burden was significantly reduced. For Alexis, the settlement provided closure and peace of mind.

Final Thoughts on Federal Loan Settlement

Settling a federal student loan is not easy, and it's not guaranteed. But for borrowers facing long-term hardship with no realistic path to full repayment, asking about settlement options is worth exploring. While it won't erase the default or missed payments from your credit report, a settlement may offer long-overdue relief and help you close a difficult chapter in your financial journey.

Offset of Income Tax Refunds

When a federal student loan goes into default, the government can take serious steps to recover the money owed—one of the most common being the Treasury Offset Program. This program allows the U.S. Department of Education to intercept your federal tax refund and apply it toward your defaulted student loan balance.

Many borrowers are caught off guard when their refund is taken. Others knowingly let it happen each year, assuming that allowing the government to keep their refund will eventually pay off the debt. While this may sound like a passive repayment plan, relying on tax refund offsets is not a good long-term strategy.

Why Tax Refund Offsets Are Not a Solution

Letting your refunds be taken year after year can actually hurt you more than it helps. Here's why:

- Your loan stays in default: As long as the loan is in default, your credit continues to suffer, and you remain ineligible for federal benefits like deferment, forbearance, income-driven repayment plans, or new student aid.

- Fees and interest continue to build: Collection fees and interest don't stop just because your refund was taken. This means your balance could grow faster than the offsets reduce it.
- You're not actively resolving the problem: Offsets are a collection method: not a repayment plan. They don't restore your loan to good standing or improve your financial record.

Example:

Destiny defaulted on her federal student loans after a long period of unemployment. She began receiving letters informing her that her tax refunds would be withheld and sure enough, for the next three years, her federal tax refunds were intercepted.

At first, Destiny was relieved she didn't have to deal with monthly payments. But over time, she realized her credit score was still low, she couldn't qualify for a mortgage, and she remained ineligible for financial aid to return to school. Worse, despite losing thousands in tax refunds, her loan balance barely moved due to the added interest and collection costs.

Eventually, Destiny entered a loan rehabilitation program. After making nine affordable monthly payments, her loan was removed from default. She got her credit back on track and became eligible for income-driven repayment options that better fit her budget. More importantly, her future tax refunds were no longer at risk for interception.

What You Can Do Instead

If you're facing tax refund offsets because of a defaulted federal loan, don't assume it's your only option. You may be eligible for:

- **Loan rehabilitation**, which removes the default from your credit

- **Loan consolidation**, which restores your loan to good standing
- **Affordable monthly payments** based on your income

These options not only stop the offsets but also help you rebuild your financial future.

SIX

Student Loans and Bankruptcy

Under current U.S. bankruptcy law, most student loans—whether federal or private—are not automatically discharged when you file for bankruptcy. This rule applies to all "qualified education loans," regardless of whether they are issued by a for-profit bank or a nonprofit lender. If, however, a borrower's other debts are either repaid or discharged through bankruptcy, it is possible for the person to find an affordable payment plan within the Federal Loan Repayment Options listed on pages 7-9.

Why Student Loans Are Treated Differently in Bankruptcy

Student loans are generally treated more strictly than other types of debt like credit cards or personal loans. This is largely due to their nature:

- They are unsecured (not backed by collateral)
- Often issued to young borrowers with no income or credit history
- Include a delayed repayment period, often years after disbursement

In the 1970s and 1980s, as default rates surged, lawmakers grew concerned about widespread abuse of bankruptcy to escape student loan repayment. In response, they passed legislation to protect lenders and stabilize the student loan system.

The most significant shift came with the *Bankruptcy Abuse Prevention and Consumer Protection Act of 2005*, which made all qualified education loans—including private loans—non-dischargeable in bankruptcy, unless the borrower can prove "undue hardship."

How to Discharge Student Loans in Bankruptcy

Although it's difficult, discharging student loans through bankruptcy is not impossible.

To do this, the borrower must:

1. **File for bankruptcy** (usually Chapter 7 or Chapter 13)
2. **File a separate legal action** within the case, known as an adversary proceeding
3. **Prove that repaying the loan would impose an "undue hardship"** on themselves and their dependents

Understanding the Brunner Test

The most common standard used by courts to evaluate undue hardship is called the **Brunner Test**, which includes three criteria:

1. **Inability to maintain a minimal standard of living** if forced to repay the loan
2. **Long-term hardship**—the financial situation is unlikely to improve during the repayment period
3. **Good faith effort to repay** the loan in the past

Historically, meeting all three elements has been very difficult. However, recent updates from the Department of Education and Department of Justice have streamlined the process, offering borrowers a more consistent and fair review of their hardship claims. A simplified application and clearer evaluation guidelines have led to more favorable outcomes.

In fact, in the first 10 months after these changes, nearly all borrowers who filed properly received full or partial discharges.

Example:

Sheronda, a 45-year-old former teacher, filed for bankruptcy after years of financial hardship. She had $82,000 in federal student loans that had been in default for over a decade. Sheronda had attempted several repayment plans, but a chronic illness forced her to stop working. She was living on Social Security Disability Insurance and had no significant assets or ability to return to work.

With the help of a bankruptcy attorney, Sheronda filed an adversary proceeding and completed the Department of Justice's new hardship attestation form. She demonstrated that:

• Her income was below the federal poverty level

• Her medical condition was permanent

• She had previously made good-faith efforts to repay the loans

After reviewing the evidence, the judge approved a full discharge of Sheronda's student loans, concluding that repayment would impose an undue hardship. The ruling brought long-awaited relief and lifted a heavy burden of financial and emotional stress from Sheronda's life.

Other Discharge and Forgiveness Options (Outside Bankruptcy)

Even if bankruptcy is not the right path for you, there are several *non-bankruptcy options* that may result in partial or total loan discharge:

- **Public Service Loan Forgiveness (PSLF):** Forgives remaining balance after 120 qualifying payments for eligible public service employees
- **Teacher Loan Forgiveness:** Offers up to $17,500 in forgiveness for eligible teachers in low-income schools
- **Total and Permanent Disability Discharge:** For borrowers who are medically determined to be unable to work
- **Closed School Discharge:** If your school closed while you were enrolled or shortly after you withdrew
- **False Certification Discharge:** If your school falsely certified your loan eligibility
- **Unpaid Refund Discharge:** If your school failed to return unused loan funds after your withdrawal
- **Discharge Due to Death:** Federal loans are discharged if the borrower (or student, for Parent PLUS loans) passes away

While Chapter 13 bankruptcy does not discharge student loans, it may offer temporary relief. Student loan payments can be included in the court-approved repayment plan, which may reduce or pause them for up to five years. However, any balance not paid off during that period will still be owed after the plan ends.

Discharging student loans through bankruptcy is rare but it is possible. If you're facing long-term hardship, especially due to disability, illness, or fixed income, it may be worth consulting a qualified bankruptcy attorney. With recent policy shifts, your chances of discharge may be better than they were just a few years ago.

SEVEN

Recent Developments in Federal Student Loan Policy

In recent years, the federal student loan system has undergone major shifts in response to political, legal, and economic pressures. These changes affect everything from repayment options and forgiveness eligibility to loan servicing and bankruptcy rights. The following summarizes the most significant updates:

Resumption of Loan Collections

As of May 2025, the U.S. Department of Education has resumed collections on defaulted federal student loans, ending the pause that began in March 2020 during the COVID-19 pandemic. Approximately 5.3 million borrowers are impacted and now face the return of wage garnishments, tax refund seizures, and Social Security offsets through the Treasury Offset Program. Borrowers in default are encouraged to explore options like loan rehabilitation or consolidation to avoid further penalties.

Policy Shifts and Legislative Proposals

The Trump administration and Republican lawmakers have introduced a series of proposals intended to overhaul the federal student loan system. These include both administrative and legislative measures aimed at restructuring repayment plans, limiting loan forgiveness eligibility, and shifting how loans are managed.

Transfer of Loan Management: The administration has proposed transferring the federal student loan portfolio—currently valued at over $1.7 trillion—from the Department of Education to the Small Business Administration (SBA). While this shift is still under review, critics question the SBA's capacity to handle such a complex system. Borrowers' repayment terms, however, would remain unchanged due to the legal obligations outlined in their original promissory notes.

Public Service Loan Forgiveness (PSLF) Restrictions: Proposed legislation would reduce PSLF eligibility by excluding medical and dental residents, as well as those in nonprofit hospital residencies, from the forgiveness program. It would also cap federal borrowing at $50,000 for undergraduate students and $100,000 for graduate students. Critics argue these changes could limit access to higher education and discourage careers in public service and healthcare.

Executive Order Revising PSLF Employment Standards: In March 2025, an executive order was signed directing the Department of Education to revise PSLF eligibility further. It instructs the Department of Education to exclude borrowers employed by organizations deemed to be involved in activities considered harmful to national interests, such as violating immigration law, promoting discrimination, or inciting public unrest. While the order does not immediately alter borrower eligibility, it signals a stricter interpretation of what qualifies as eligible public service employment and has raised concerns about potential bias against advocacy-based nonprofits and civil rights organizations.

Changes to Income-Driven Repayment Plans

Several income-driven repayment (IDR) plans—SAVE, PAYE, and ICR—have been paused pending legal review. These plans were created through administrative action rather than congressional legislation, prompting questions about their long-term legality. Borrowers enrolled in these plans have been placed in interest-free forbearance, but their paused payments do not count toward PSLF. The only IDR plan currently active for forgiveness purposes is the Income-Based Repayment (IBR) plan, which is grounded in federal statute.

Separately, recent reforms to IBR have improved borrower protections by lowering monthly payments to 10 percent of discretionary income (down from 15 percent) and allowing forgiveness after 20 years of qualifying payments instead of 25. These updates may offer limited relief but do not affect private loans.

Bankruptcy and Student Loan Discharge

Effective July 1, 2024, borrowers in Chapter 13 bankruptcy may now receive credit toward loan forgiveness under IDR and PSLF programs. Even if no direct student loan payments are made during the bankruptcy period, each month of compliance with the Chapter 13 repayment plan counts toward forgiveness. Borrowers should coordinate with their bankruptcy attorneys and loan servicers to ensure their repayment plans qualify.

There is also renewed legislative interest in expanding bankruptcy protections for student loan borrowers. Past efforts include:

- **H.R. 532 – Private Student Loan Bankruptcy Fairness Act of 2013**, which proposed allowing private student loans to be discharged in bankruptcy

- **S. 114 – Fairness for Struggling Students Act of 2013,** which aimed to permit discharge of both federal and private loans if repayment posed an undue hardship

While these bills failed to pass at the time, growing public concern over student loan debt has brought the issue back into the spotlight. Future legislation may build on these foundations to provide more meaningful relief for struggling borrowers.

2025 Legislative Update: What You Need to Know

In July 2025, sweeping changes to federal student loans were enacted under the "One Big Beautiful Bill." This law overhauls repayment options, borrowing limits, and forgiveness timelines, particularly for new borrowers on or after July 1, 2026. If you're an existing borrower, many of the programs explained in this book still apply. But if you're taking out new loans—or advising someone who is—it's important to understand what's changing.

Programs Being Phased Out

Borrowers before July 1, 2026 may still qualify for the repayment plans described throughout this book. These include:

SAVE (Saving on a Valuable Education Plan):

This plan caps payments at 5 percent of discretionary income for undergraduate loans. It offers early forgiveness after 10 to 25 years depending on loan balance and prevents unpaid interest from accumulating, meaning monthly balances don't grow even when payments are low.

PAYE (Pay As You Earn):

PAYE limits monthly payments to 10 percent of discretionary income and provides forgiveness after 20 years. It is only available to borrowers who took out loans after October 2007 and received a disbursement after October 2011.

IBR (Income-Based Repayment):

For newer borrowers, monthly payments are capped at 10 percent of discretionary income; for older borrowers, it's 15 percent. Forgiveness is available after 20 to 25 years, depending on when the borrower took out loans. Qualification also requires demonstrating partial financial hardship.

ICR (Income-Contingent Repayment):

This plan calculates payments as the lesser of 20 percent of discretionary income or a fixed 12-year payment adjusted to income. Forgiveness occurs after 25 years. It is also available to Parent PLUS borrowers who consolidate into a Direct Loan. These plans are being eliminated for new borrowers starting July 1, 2026.

What's Replacing Them

New borrowers will be limited to just two repayment options: the Standard 10-Year Planand the Repayment Assistance Plan (RAP).

Standard 10-Year Plan

This plan features fixed monthly payments based on loan size and interest rate. There is no forgiveness—loans are fully paid off in 10 years. While this option often results in the highest monthly payments, it is also the fastest path to becoming debt-free.

Marcus' Story

Marcus graduated with $42,000 in federal loans and started a job earning $65,000. He chose the Standard 10-Year Plan, paying around $450 per month. It was a stretch, but he budgeted tightly and avoided extra debt. By year eight, he was nearly done, and by year ten, completely free from student loans. This plan worked well for him because he had a steady income and wanted to be done with debt quickly.

Repayment Assistance Plan (RAP)

RAP determines monthly payments based on income, but it is not as generous as SAVE or PAYE. Forgiveness occurs after 30 years regardless of loan balance, but interest accrues during repayment and may not be subsidized. This means borrowers could see their balances grow even while making payments.

Jasmin's Story

Jasmin graduated with $92,000 in loans and took a nonprofit job earning $52,000. She enrolled in RAP with payments starting around $180 per month. After five years, her balance had barely changed—interest had pushed her loan to over $98,000. Forgiveness would come after 30 years, but the debt felt permanent. To add to the concern, Jasmin could also be facing a tax bill for the forgiven amount, depending on future IRS regulations. While RAP allowed her to afford payments today, the long-term cost was far higher.

These examples show the contrast between short-term affordability and long-term impact. Borrowers must weigh these factors carefully when choosing a repayment path.

Deferment and Forbearance Changes

Current borrowers still have access to economic hardship deferment, unemployment deferment, and up to 36 months of forbearance. However, under the new law, these protections are being reduced for new borrowers.

Deferment for economic hardship or unemployment will no longer be available to borrowers who take out loans after July 1, 2027. Forbearance will be limited to a total of nine months within any two-year period. Instead, borrowers will be directed toward RAP as the alternative to pausing payments.

Why This Matters

These changes make federal loans stricter and less forgiving, especially for future graduate students and parents. This book was written to help borrowers navigate the current system, and that guidance still applies if your loans were disbursed before July 1, 2026.

But if you are borrowing after that date—or supporting someone who is—it's essential to understand that repayment flexibility is shrinking. Interest may accumulate more quickly under RAP, forgiveness timelines are being extended from 20 or 25 years to 30 years, and access to graduate and PLUS loans will be capped or eliminated altogether.

Looking Ahead

These developments represent a significant shift in the student loan landscape. Borrowers are strongly encouraged to stay informed about changes, review their repayment strategies, and consult with financial advisors, loan servicers or legal experts when navigating new policies. Whether pursuing forgiveness, facing default, or considering bankruptcy, understanding the evolving legal and policy environment is critical to making informed decisions.

Maybe you borrowed the money with hope. Maybe you signed the papers with questions. Or maybe you just did what you had to do, trusting you'd figure it out along the way. Either way, you're here now — stronger, more informed, and ready to move forward.

Student loan debt can feel like a setback, but it doesn't have to define your future. Now you understand how the system works.

You know what to look out for, and you've gained the tools to take charge of your path.

You don't need to have it all figured out today. Just take the next right step. Even small steps matter. Keep asking questions. Keep showing up for yourself.

Keep moving forward.

Appendix A: Resources

To assist borrowers in navigating these changes, the Federal Student Aid (FSA) office offers several tools:

- **Loan Simulator:** This tool helps borrowers estimate monthly payments and compare different repayment plans based on their income and loan details.
- **Aidan Virtual Assistant:** Aidan is an AI-powered assistant that can answer questions about federal student aid, helping borrowers understand their options and manage their loans effectively.

Appendix B:
Student Loan Debt Management Updates (2025)

Repayment Options Overview

1. **SAVE Plan (Saving on a Valuable Education)**
   - Capped at 5–10% of discretionary income.
   - Forgiveness after 10–25 years depending on balance.
   - Currently blocked by federal courts.
2. **PAYE (Pay As You Earn)**
   - 10% of discretionary income.
   - Forgiveness after 20 years.
   - Requires financial hardship.
3. **ICR (Income-Contingent Repayment)**
   - 20% of discretionary income or 12-year fixed plan amount.
   - Forgiveness after 25 years.
   - Only IDR plan available for Parent PLUS Loans (after consolidation).
4. **Repayment Assistance Plan (Proposed)**
   - Would replace current IDR options.
   - Forgiveness after 30 years.
   - Proposed by House Republicans.

Bankruptcy Considerations (Effective July 1, 2024)

1. **IDR & PSLF Credit Under Chapter 13**
   - Monthly trustee payments count toward forgiveness.
   - No need for adversary proceeding.
   - Applies to borrowers actively in Chapter 13 repayment.
2. **Implications**
   - Easier path to forgiveness for bankruptcy filers.

- Recognition of good-faith repayment efforts.

Public Service Loan Forgiveness (PSLF) Changes

1. **Program Status**
   - Still active under Trump administration.
   - Stricter employer eligibility (excludes certain nonprofits).
2. **Eligibility Requirements**
   - 120 qualifying payments.
   - Full-time work for a qualifying employer.
   - Direct Loan enrollment and use of qualifying repayment plan.
3. **IDR Account Adjustment (One-Time Credit)**
   - Credits for prior forbearance and deferment periods.
   - Especially helpful for PSLF applicants.
   - Deadline to consolidate FFEL/Perkins: June 30, 2024.

Legislative and Administrative Policy Changes

1. **Loan Type Caps and Restrictions**
   - Proposed caps: $50,000 for undergrads, $100,000 for grads.
   - End to Grad PLUS loans.
2. **Colleges Held Financially Accountable**
   - Institutions could pay a portion of defaulted loans.
3. **PSLF Restrictions**
   - Exclusion of certain types of nonprofits and public interest employers.
4. **Resumption of Collections**
   - Collections restarted May 2025 after the pandemic pause.
   - Affecting ~5 million borrowers.

Key Resources and Tools

1. **Loan Simulator**: https://studentaid.gov/loan-simulator
   - Helps compare repayment plans.
2. **Aidan Virtual Assistant**: https://studentaid.gov/aidan
   - AI tool for answering questions and guiding borrowers.
3. **PSLF Help Tool**: https://studentaid.gov/pslf/
   - Check employer eligibility and track forgiveness progress.

Legal and Advocacy Resources

1. **Federal Student Aid**: https://studentaid.gov
2. **National Consumer Law Center**: https://www.nclc.org
3. **Student Borrower Protection Center**: https://protectborrowers.org

Note: This appendix reflects laws and proposals current as of May 2025. Borrowers should consult with their loan servicer, a qualified legal advisor, or financial counselor for the most up-to-date guidance.